# Facts About Sex

## for Today's Youth

## SOL GORDON

Illustrated by Vivien Cohen

Prometheus Books
Buffalo, New York

Published 1992 by Prometheus Books.

96 95 94 93 92     5 4 3 2 1

Library of Congress Cataloging-in-Publication Data

Gordon, Sol, 1923–
    Facts about sex for today's youth / Sol Gordon : illustrated by Vivien Cohen.
        p.    cm.
    Originally published: New ed. Fayetteville, N.Y. : Ed-U Press, 1987.
    Includes bibliographical references.
    Summary: A simple discussion of various aspects of sexual maturation, including definitions of vulgar or slang terms in reference to sex and sexual organs.
    ISBN 0-87975-771-X
    1. Sex instruction for youth. [1. Sex instruction for youth.] I. Cohen, Vivien, ill. II. Title.
[HQ35.G65    1992]
306.7'07—dc20                                                              92-6730
                                                                              CIP
                                                                              AC

Printed in the United States of America on acid-free paper.

# Contents

## The Author

Sol Gordon is a clinical psychologist. He has taught courses in child and adolescent psychology at the University of Pennsylvania, Rutgers University and Yeshiva University. Dr. Gordon is the author of the introductory text *Psychology For You,* and has had many articles published in professional journals. He is Professor Emeritus of Child and Family Studies at Syracuse University, New York.

## The Illustrator

Vivien Cohen obtained her B.A. from Pratt Institute, School of Fine and Applied Arts. She has had extensive training and experience as a medical artist. She resides in Woodbridge, New Jersey.

# Author's Introduction

Parents are not always clear on how much their children know—or should know—about sex. Most parents have a tough time when they discuss topics like sexual intercourse and masturbation. As a result, most young people learn about sex from their friends, through the medium of curse words, dirty jokes, graffiti and the distorted and exaggerated views of sex conveyed by television, movies and newspapers.

Many parents feel that knowing "too much" too early leads to sexual misbehavior, but most experts have the opposite view. Children are much more likely to have sexual difficulties if they don't know what sex is all about. Even pornography is not necessarily harmful. Young people who are well informed about sex usually find pornography boring or repulsive.

It is very important for young people to understand sex and to know the language associated with it, including "street" expressions which we have used in a few instances to explain the meaning of difficult words. If teenagers remain uninformed, they tend to be insecure, and are more susceptible to irresponsible behavior.

Adolescents are particularly preoccupied with thoughts about sex because they are experiencing physical and emotional changes. While some behavior can be abnormal, all thoughts, fantasies, dreams and ideas—even if they are about sexual exploits—are normal. People sometimes have thoughts, impulses or dreams which worry them. The more they worry about them, the more often the thoughts recur. It is important to understand that this happens because of guilt feelings. If they knew that all of us have sexual thoughts and desires, they would be less concerned about their own.

Children may want to discuss some of their sexual concerns with their parents. Parents should be able to accept such confidences without making their children feel guilty.

Those of you who have teenage children should read this entire book. Parents of younger children should also read it to prepare themselves for the questions their children will someday ask. If you're not ready with answers, they will ask elsewhere. Although written for adolescents, some ten and eleven-year-olds can profit from this book. The worst that could happen to young children who read it is that they might not understand everything.

Do not be deceived when your child says he or she is not interested in learning about sex. Few boys are willing to admit to adults that they do not know all there is to know about sex, and few girls are willing to admit that they are even interested in sex. If you feel your child is not ready to acknowledge this interest, just leave the book around so he or she can read it privately.

This book is purposely brief because the average young person to whom it is addressed will not read, or may get confused by, a long, detailed or "moralistic" presentation. Most books about sex are written to please uptight parents. It is little wonder that despite the availability of hundreds of sex education books, they are read by relatively few young people.

We hope you will find *Facts About Sex* a starting point for meaningful communication about the larger and **more important** role of values as it relates to sex and family living. This book does make some judgments and includes some controversial issues. We hope that parents will feel free to discuss their own views in a manner that will help their children appreciate the fact that differences of opinion exist in every vital area of human interaction.

In this new edition, it is essential to note the findings of recent research which show that many (if not most) teenagers will have sex before marriage without parental knowledge or consent. We are merely acknowledging the trend; we do not advocate this behavior. As a matter of fact, this book outlines good reasons why teenagers should *not* engage in sexual intercourse. However, in view of the existing facts, we must consider the question—is it not better to use birth control than to bring an unwanted child into this world? Remember too, youths need models, not critics.

3

# Sex—
# In Plain Language

You will read and hear a lot about sex. People talk about it and many television programs emphasize sex in some way. Sex is both emotional and physical. Some people think that the physical part of sex is dirty. They are wrong. Most people, however, feel that sexual acts should be conducted in private by consenting adults. This is what we think as well.

When people talk about sex appeal, they usually mean being attractive to the opposite sex. When they talk about "sleeping together," "getting laid," "having sex," "having relations," they usually mean sexual intercourse. Another word for sexual intercourse is coitus. There are several "vulgar" words for sexual intercourse. Ordinary words like "ball," "jump," "making it" and "screw" are also used as impolite ways of referring to sexual intercourse.

# Sexual
# Intercourse

Sexual intercourse occurs when a man puts his enlarged (erect) penis into the vagina* of a

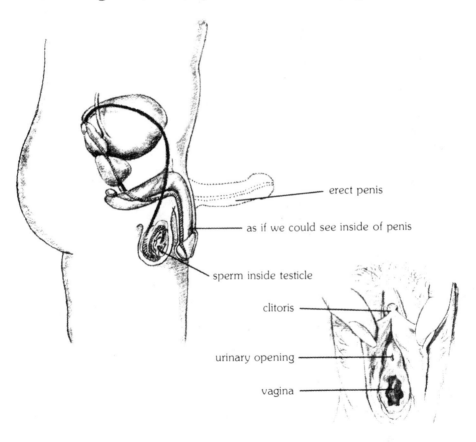

erect penis

as if we could see inside of penis

sperm inside testicle

clitoris

urinary opening

vagina

*Some "street" words for vagina are "box," "snatch," "cunt," "hole," "pussy." It is not polite to use any of these expressions.

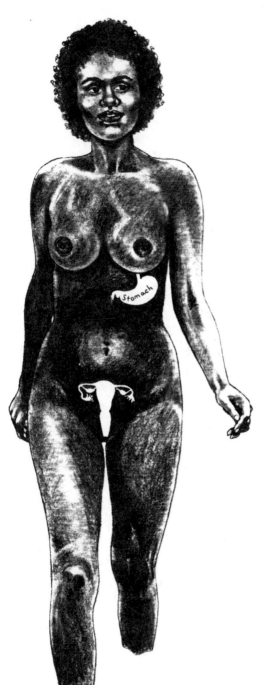

This is the way the sperm from the male (shown greatly enlarged) travels within the woman's body to reach the egg after intercourse takes place.

This is the way the fertilized egg cell grows to become a baby.

6

woman. Boys sometimes wonder about the chance of urine accidentally coming through the penis while intercourse is taking place. Nature takes care of that. Urine cannot come out during intercourse. The release of the sperm into the vagina is called ejaculation (e-jack-u-lay-shun). After the man ejaculates (comes), the penis loses its erection. It takes a while before the penis can become erect again.

One position for sexual intercourse is when the woman lies on her back and the man lies on top, facing her. However, couples who feel like it vary their positions during sexual relations. Sometimes one partner is more active than the other. No particular position, if it is voluntary and enjoyable, is considered "better" or more "normal" than another.

Before, during and after sexual intercourse, a couple will usually kiss, embrace and stroke each other to show their affection.

# Human Reproduction

Human reproduction refers to the creation of a new human being. Most living things, including animals

This is what an unborn fetus looks like as it develops inside the mother's uterus. This picture is shown as though you could see inside the mother's body.

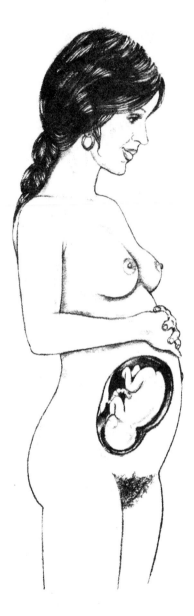

About halfway
through pregnancy

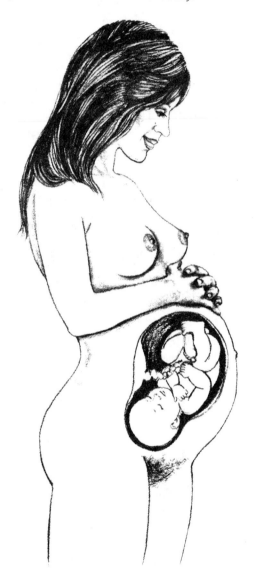

Just before
the **baby** is born

and plants, need a male and female to reproduce. Human beings can reproduce after they reach puberty. Puberty is the time when a boy is able to produce sperm and to make a girl pregnant and the girl is able to have children. After the female reaches puberty, at a certain time of each month, she produces within her body a tiny egg cell called the ovum. After sexual intercourse, if a sperm unites with the egg cell, it is called fertilization. If the fertilized cell attaches to the wall of the uterus, the woman becomes pregnant. This means a fetus is being developed. The place inside the female where it develops is called the uterus.* Womb is another name for the uterus. The baby is called an embryo in the first three months of pregnancy, and a fetus in the remaining months. A full term pregnancy usually lasts nine months. Sometimes a fetus is expelled from the uterus before it has fully developed. This is called a miscarriage.

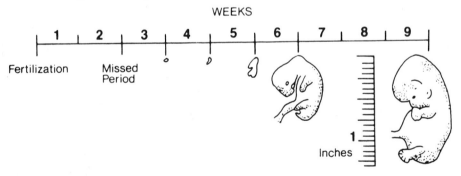

The growth of the embryo (actual sizes). All but a small percentage of miscarriages and abortions occur during the first nine weeks of pregnancy.

*Although people will often speak of the fetus developing in the woman's stomach, this is not correct. The fetus remains in the uterus until birth.

Childbirth as seen from outside:

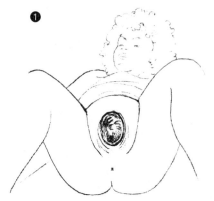

1. Top of baby's head shows ("crowns")

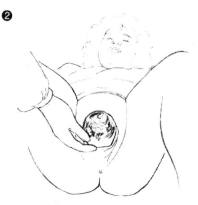

2. head is coming out

3. head is out

4. head turns. Mucus is removed with bulb syringe

5. shoulders come out

Newborn baby is usually wrinkled and puffy. A white cheeselike substance covers the baby (vernix).

10

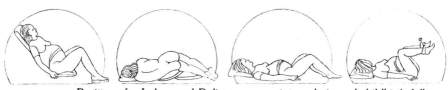

Positions for Labor and Delivery          internal view of childbirth follows:

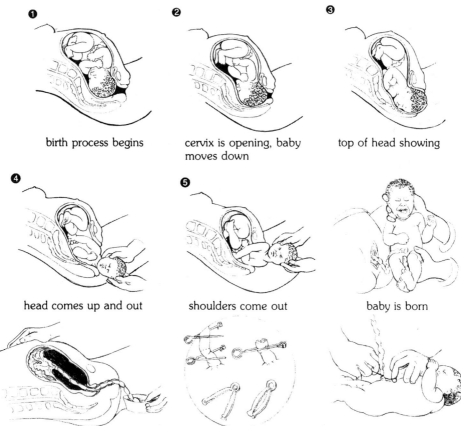

**❶** birth process begins

**❷** cervix is opening, baby moves down

**❸** top of head showing

**❹** head comes up and out

**❺** shoulders come out

baby is born

labor cont. (uterus goes on squeezing) until placenta or afterbirth comes out

two types of clamps

cord is tied and cut

11

A woman knows she is ready to give birth when she feels muscle contractions in the uterus every 5-10 minutes. This is the signal that she will soon begin "labor"—the process of giving birth. It is called "labor" because the woman must work hard to push the baby down the birth canal so it can be born.

At birth the baby comes out, usually head first, through the vagina, which stretches as the baby is being born. Most children are born without physical handicaps, although sometimes injury to the brain or other parts of the body can occur during birth. Birth defects can also occur as a result of carelessness. Smoking, poor diet, alcohol, and some drugs can cause damage in the newborn. Prenatal (during pregnancy) care is very important for the health of the baby and for its mother. In addition, research has shown that a pregnant girl under eighteen faces higher risks medically. The younger the girl the greater the risk for both the mother and the new born child. The chances of a teenager giving birth to a premature or mentally retarded baby are much greater than if she gave birth in her early twenties.

# The
# Male

**M**ost boys are developed sexually (reach puberty) between ages 12 and 15. Some reach puberty a little sooner, and some a little later. A boy will develop hair under his arms and around his genitals (sex organs).* The genitals are the penis ("dick," "prick," and "cock" are the street words for this organ) and the testicles ("balls" or "nuts" are the slang words.)

As a young man develops sexually, his penis becomes enlarged and erect (hard) once in a while, sometimes when he is thinking about sex and sometimes for no reason he can figure out. This happens to all males.

Boys often refer to their enlarged penis as an "erection," a "boner," or a "hard on." Whether erect or not, the size of the penis is not important. The size of the penis does not affect sexual pleasure.

---

*The hair around the sex organs is called "pubic hair" because the area around the sex organs is called the "pubis."

13

Along with its capacity to become enlarged and harder, the penis, when stimulated, will at times release semen—a whitish, sticky fluid which contains the sperm. (The sperm are produced in the testicles.) Both males and females can become sexually stimulated or excited by their thoughts, day or night dreams, by looking at "sexy" pictures, by touching or rubbing their genitals, by making love and in many other ways. The most intense pleasure from sexual stimulation (in males and females) is called an orgasm (climax).

To ejaculate (to release semen) is sometimes called "to come." When you are asleep and semen comes out, this is referred to as a nocturnal emission or a "wet dream." It is normal, and you should not worry about getting your underclothes or sheets messy. Parents know that this happens to all adolescent boys.

Male and female reproductive cells.

Sperm

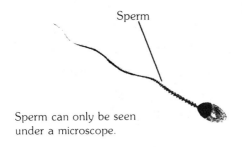

Sperm can only be seen under a microscope.

A single ejaculation contains millions of sperm.

Ovum (female egg)

The female egg cell is the size of a grain of sand.

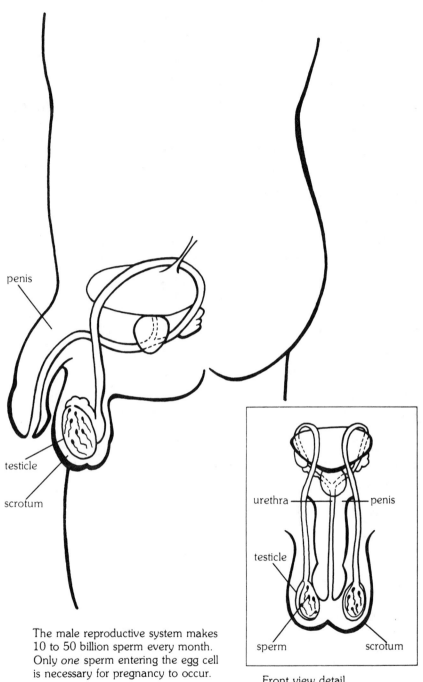

penis

testicle

scrotum

The male reproductive system makes
10 to 50 billion sperm every month.
Only *one* sperm entering the egg cell
is necessary for pregnancy to occur.

urethra — penis

testicle

sperm scrotum

Front view detail
of male reproductive organs.

15

Most boys enjoy rubbing or stimulating their penises because it is pleasurable and it helps reduce sexual tension. This is called masturbation, which sometimes results in an ejaculation. In language that is not polite, it is called "jerking off," "beating your meat," "whacking off," "jacking off" and a few other names.

Although some will deny it, almost all boys masturbate at one time or another. It is normal. As with all forms of sexual activity, masturbation should be done in private. Masturbation is not physically harmful even if done often. However, like everything else that is done "too much,"* it begins to lose its attraction and pleasure. If masturbation becomes "compulsive," which means a habit you can't control, then it is probably a sign of distress.

Many sexual thoughts and fantasies occur to boys when they masturbate. Just because you think of something, it doesn't mean you should or would do it. Sometimes in a fit of anger we think of wanting to hurt somebody; but that doesn't mean we are going to do it. At times we think about having sexual intercourse with someone we know, even a close family member, but that doesn't mean we are seriously considering it.

*People usually ask, "How much is too much?" The answer is "once is too much if you don't enjoy it." Masturbation is a normal sexual expression for both males and females at any age.

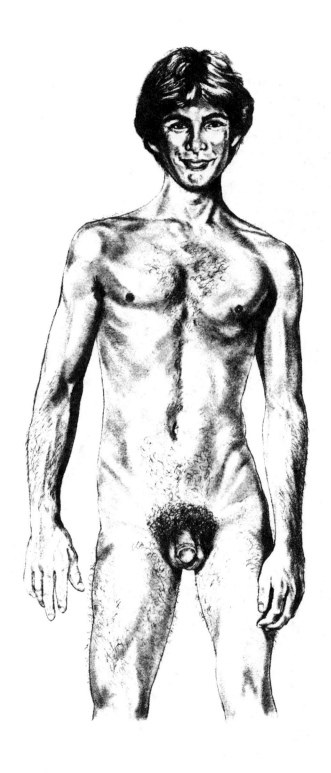

This is a sexually developed young man.

This is a sexually developed young woman.

When people marry, they may give up masturbation. Husbands and wives have sexual intercourse as a way of expressing love for each other, for pleasure, as well as for having children. This does not mean, however, that there is anything wrong with masturbation after marriage. When opportunities for sexual intercourse are not readily available, such as during a long period of absence or the later stages of pregnancy, masturbation is a normal way of satisfying sexual needs. Some people occasionally masturbate even when sexual intercourse is available because they enjoy the experience.

# The
# Female

Girls develop sexually earlier than boys—usually when they are about 10 or 11 years old, but some girls do not develop until they are 15 or 16 years old. Being developed sexually for a girl means she is able to become pregnant; her breasts increase in size, pubic hair grows around her vulva; and she begins to have her "period." The "period" (menstruation) lasts for a few days each month. This occurs in females who are not pregnant. When a woman is menstruating, blood-enriched tissue is discharged through the vagina. When a girl has her period, she wears a protective sanitary pad or tampon for her comfort and to prevent her clothing from being stained. Some women feel slightly ill or moody, or have cramps just before or during menstruation, but most engage in regular activities. A girl should shower or bathe daily during her period to prevent body odor. Some people refer to menstruation as their "friend," the "curse," being "on the rag," or being "unwell," but menstruation is not a sickness.

Many girls enjoy stimulating their genital areas because it is pleasurable and helps reduce sexual tension. This is called masturbation. Often a fluid is slowly discharged in the vagina. The clitoris is a source of sexual pleasure for the woman both in masturbation and during intercourse. Masturbation among females is normal, and is a problem only if it becomes "compulsive." If it is something you can't control, masturbation can increase sexual tension rather than reduce it. All sorts of thoughts and fantasies occur to girls when they are sexually stimulated.

The size and rate of growth of the breasts differs from girl to girl. A girl might notice that one breast is larger than the other—this often happens. Large or small, the size of a girl's breasts has nothing to do with her personal maturity or her sexuality.

# What Is
# Love?

Young people often wonder if they are really "in love." You can love many people: your parents, friends, relatives, and others. Being "in love" usually refers to a powerful desire to be with and to please another person. When you are in love, you will want to have the respect and affection of the person you love. Although you may not always agree with that person's opinions, if you are in love, the two of you will settle your differences without trying to hurt each other. You will want him or her to be proud of you.

Some young people say they are in love, but at the same time neglect their studies or work, or become careless about their appearance and their actions when they are with the person they supposedly love. They try to attract attention by neglecting their health or taking foolish risks. Experience will show that this may be a "crush," sexual attraction, or immature attachment. It is also common among young people to "love" or hero-worship popular schoolmates and teachers as well as famous people whom they have never met. Real love is a shared intimacy, based on mutual respect and affection.

Sexual intercourse or sexual attraction is not the most important part of a loving relationship.

Of course, young people must also be able to accept disappointments. Sometimes you will fall in love with a person who does not return your love. If the other person doesn't show that he or she feels the same way after a reasonable time, you should look for someone else. Some adolescents think that being in love happens only once in a lifetime. This is not true. It is possible to be in love many times.

This may sound strange, but people who are involved in immature love affairs are often tired for no apparent reason. Those who are into the *real thing* are energized by the relationship. Check this out with your friends.

Please remember that it is possible to be sexually turned on by someone you don't like much. In the long run, the best sexual experiences emerge slowly with a person you really care about.

# Sex
# Before Marriage

**M**any young people have sexual relations before marriage (premarital sex). However, when sex is not related to love, it is often unsatisfying and can lead to emotional problems. One problem is the risk of unwanted pregnancy. Some girls have an abortion, which means ending a pregnancy in its early stages. Abortion, however, is an extremely dangerous operation *if not done by a doctor.* * It is sad to report that only about 20% of young people use any reliable form of contraception the first time they have sexual intercourse.

Another problem with premarital sex is the risk of venereal disease (VD or as it is now commonly termed, STD—Sexually Transmitted Disease). Gonorrhea (sometimes called "clap") and chlamydia are two very serious venereal diseases. Most types of VD are curable if discovered early and treated by a doctor. Unfortunately, the symptoms in women are not obvious; they don't always know they have it. A boy or girl can get VD the first time he or she has sexual contact with another person. Even more serious is the fact that AIDS—a relatively new sexually transmitted and fatal disease—is rapidly spreading throughout the world. No cure for it has been found as of late 1992.

*Abortions early in pregnancy are simple and safe if done by a physician. If a teenager becomes pregnant, a medical abortion may be more moral than bringing an unwanted child into the world.

24

Sometimes a boy will say to a girl, "If you do not have sex with me, I won't take you out anymore." Any girl who has sex with such a boy is not very smart. He is not interested in the girl as a person, and in many cases the boy will not see the girl again after they have had sexual relations. Be on the alert for boys (and girls too) who use *lines* to get you to have sex. For example, "If you really loved me . . ." Why not respond by saying, "If you really loved me, you wouldn't put this kind of pressure on me."

There are many ways for adolescents and young adults to deal with their strong and healthy sexual urges without having sexual intercourse. Some of these are dating (which could involve kissing, necking and petting, often called "making out"\*), masturbation, thinking and dreaming about sex, talking about it with a close friend, reading about it, discussing and kidding about sex in a group, or looking at magazines like *Playboy* and *Playgirl*. Young persons who are overly worried about sex and who neglect their work at school, their chores, etc., are probably feeling guilty about sex. Remember that all dreams, thoughts, and urges about sex are normal. Once you truly understand this, any *unpleasant* sexual thoughts and urges you have will last only a short while, and will not be very upsetting. (Of course, you may want to fully enjoy the *pleasurable* sexual thoughts and feelings that you get.)

---

\*Intense physical contact with a person you don't really care about, however, is often not a pleasant experience. It could lead to an increase of tension rather than provide an outlet for sexual urges.

Some people boast a lot about sex. In most cases, they are either not telling the truth or they suffer from feelings of inferiority. Sometimes groups of boys or girls discuss sex among themselves. This will not be an embarrassing situation for those who know the facts.

## Sex Problems

There are youth and adults who have serious sexual problems. Some have sexual relations with children. This is always wrong and harmful. There are men who are so disturbed that they force others to have sex with them. This is called rape. A woman or a man who has sexual intercourse with another person for money is called a prostitute.

Some men may find that they are impotent (unable to have an erection when they want to have intercourse), or they may ejaculate prematurely ("come" before or immediately upon putting the penis into the vagina). Some women don't enjoy sex, or even if they do, they don't have an orgasm. For both men and women, this may be a temporary situation. Too much alcohol or drugs often results in sexual problems. Sex problems could also be due to guilt, inexperience, or unfavorable conditions often associated with first experiences with sex. Occasionally, it may be due to a physical problem. It can also be the result of the partner not being sensitive enough about her (or his) sexual and emotional needs. Sexual difficulties of this kind are usually solved when two people work at their problems with love and understanding for each other. If problems persist, professional help should be sought.

Some people are "always on the make," which means that they often talk about and want to have sex with someone, but they are not really interested in that someone as a person. Young people "on the make," whether they know it or not, fear and dislike the opposite sex. Because they are unsure about their own sexuality they think they can "prove" something by having many sexual experiences. The fact is that no matter how often they have sex, they are rarely satisfied, even though they may make fun of others who are not yet "experienced."

In any case, sexual intercourse by itself is never a test or a proof of love. It can be and often is an aspect of a loving relationship. It can also be an expression of violence (as in rape) or hostility (as when it is used to exploit another person).

## HEALTH ALERT
Due to the AIDS crisis, anal and oral sex are not considered safe, especially for homosexuals, bisexuals and their partners. Anal and vaginal intercourse and oral sex should be avoided by heterosexuals who are unsure of the fidelity of their sexual partners or whose partners are intravenous drug users.

# Sex Differences

**M**any young people would like to remain virgins until marriage and some remain celibate (do not have sexual intercourse) their entire life. Both of these options are normal. These days people are considering such choices as remaining single (without excluding sex) and marrying, but without having children.

Some people prefer to have sexual experiences with persons of their own sex. They are called homosexuals.* Most boys and girls have homosexual thoughts occasionally. Some even have homosexual experiences. This doesn't mean that they are homosexual. The people properly called homosexuals are those who, as adults, have sexual contacts *only* with persons of their own sex.

Homosexual behavior is illegal in some states of the union, but most religious and professional groups are opposed to laws which interfere with the private sexual behavior between consenting adults. Some people enjoy sexual relations with both sexes throughout their adult life. They are called bisexuals. Modern psychologists no longer see homosexual or bisexual behavior between consenting adults as a disorder.

---

*The popular words for male homosexuals is "gay" and for females, "lesbians". Some negative expressions for gay men are "faggot," "fruit," and "queer;" and for females, "dyke."

# Prevention of Pregnancy

There are several ways in which women can prevent pregnancy when they have sexual intercourse. One way is to take birth control pills which are prescribed by a doctor. They must be taken regularly. Some people think that if you take the "pill" once or twice it is enough. This is not true. The "pill" is one type of contraceptive,* and is widely used for birth control and family planning. Pills are not suitable for everyone, and that is why they should be taken only under medical supervision. Another method of birth control is a device known as a diaphragm. A woman must be fitted for a diaphragm by a doctor, who will show her how to place it in the vagina. The diaphragm prevents the sperm from reaching the ovum (egg cell). A diaphragm must be used with a contraceptive jelly or cream, or it will not be effective. Another birth control method is the IUD (Intrauterine Device). It is inserted by a doctor and remains in the uterus until the doctor is asked to remove it. Contraceptive foams for women (inserted into the vagina before sexual intercourse) are available in drugstores without a prescription.

Douching and feminine hygiene products are *not* birth controls.

*A contraceptive is a device used for the purpose of preventing pregnancy. While contraceptives "work" most of the time, they are not 100 percent effective.

A man can also use a contraceptive. It is called a condom (rubber) which is available without a prescription at a drugstore (and in some states from a vending machine). It is sometimes called a "safety" or a "Trojan." A condom is a contraceptive that also helps prevent VD. The rubber is rolled onto the erect penis just before intercourse; thus, the sperm goes into the rubber instead of the vagina. When the man pulls his penis out of the vagina he should hold onto the rubber so that it does not slip off. Rubbers should be used only once. The male use of the condom combined with the female use of contraceptive foam is a good form of birth control, especially when other medical methods are not available. Another approach is for the man to pull his penis out of the vagina (withdrawal) before he comes. This is generally not "safe" and it is not sexually satisfying, but it is certainly better than no method at all. It is not romantic or spontaneous to have sex without birth control—it's stupid!

## Questions About Sex

Of the thousands of questions about sex that high school students asked me, the following ten were the most common.

## 1. Do you think it's right to have sexual intercourse at our ages . . . 15, 16, 17 . . .?

I have already suggested that it is not a good idea, and I am sure this answer will not satisfy some readers. I think it's wrong for teenagers to risk pregnancy, venereal disease, or to make immature decisions because of confusing crushes and infatuations. In addition, sexual intercourse with a person you don't love or respect is seldom satisfying and can result in sexual problems. Older working or college youth who love each other and can easily arrange for contraceptives and privacy may want to make their own decisions about premarital sex. We hope that their decisions will be based on mutual respect.

Some young people feel that they have already made mistakes because of sex experiments. They need worry *only* if they have not profited from their experiences. We all make mistakes sometimes. Of course, we have to be especially careful when other people can be hurt. At the same time, we should not exaggerate the meaning of all sexual "mistakes." It is possible during adolescence to have sexual experiences with the opposite or the same sex without any undesirable effects. My point, though, is that the risk of unhappy or even tragic consequences is great. It is also sad to note that most boys—as many as 85%—will eventually abandon the teenage girls they make pregnant and even the girls they marry.

## 2. Does "jerking off" frequently cause any harmful effects later?

"Jerking off" (masturbation), no matter how frequently it is done, does not cause any physical harm. The shame or guilt that some people feel about it is what can be harmful. It is absolutely *not true*, as some people claim, that masturbation can cause insanity, acne or blindness, or that boys can use up sperm that is essential for reproduction later on. The male testes produce all the sperm needed, no matter how frequently a person masturbates.

## 3. Can a girl become pregnant when she has intercourse for the first time?

Yes. There is no absolutely "safe" time for having sexual intercourse without risking pregnancy. The risk is greatly reduced with contraception. In addition, a woman whose periods are regular is less likely to become pregnant during her menstrual period or two or three days before or after it.

## 4. Is there a way of telling what is normal or abnormal sex between two people?

This is a difficult question, but I will give you my opinion. If we assume the people involved are ready for sexual experiences, sexual "acts" can be considered "normal" ("mature" might be a better word) if the following conditions exist:

The behavior is voluntary. A person chooses to do it and it isn't something a person does because he can't help it.

The behavior is enjoyable and both partners consent to it. Birth control is used if a baby is not planned.

The behavior is not exploitive. It is free of guilt and serves to enrich the relationship. *

**5. How can you tell if you have a sexually transmitted disease (STD)?**

Venereal disease results from having sexual or close physical relations with a person (homosexual or heterosexual) who is infected. An individual most likely to spread VD is one who is promiscuous (a person who has sexual relations with many people). Three common venereal diseases are gonorrhea, syphilis, and genital herpes.

The first sign of gonorrhea for men and women often is a burning sensation in the sex organ when urinating. This would be noticed about two to six or more days after sexual relations with an infected person. Pus often drips from the penis. One of the big problems is that many women (and some men) do not have obvious symptoms and are unaware that they have gonorrhea.

The first sign of syphilis is a single sore (usually around the genitals), followed by a rash on any part of the body, appearing from ten days to as much as three months after contact. While these signs may disappear, they will soon be replaced by fever, headache and sore throat. Untreated gonorrhea and syphilis infections, despite eventual disappearance of outside signs, remain active in the body and can be the cause of sterility, blindness, insanity, and other crippling conditions. Syphilis can also result in death. Most venereal diseases, when discovered early and treated by a doctor, can be cured.

*See Health Alert, page 27.

Herpes causes painful blisters on the genitals or anus. Except for pregnant women, it is not as serious as gonorrhea or syphilis, but causes much discomfort.

Male use of the condom (rubber) and both partners urinating and washing with soap and warm water immediately after intercourse will reduce the risk of VD. With more than three million new cases each year, VD has become the most serious communicable (catching) disease in this country. All states permit clinics, Planned Parenthood Centers and private physicians to test for and treat VD without parental knowledge or consent. Doctors should be told what types of sexual activity were involved so that proper tests can be made.

## 6. How long is the average-size penis?

The average size of an erect penis (a "hard on") is between five and six inches. Actually, it does not matter whether the penis is more or less than "average." The notion that size is important for satisfactory sexual relations is not true. Some males make judgments about size by comparing their nonerect penis with others they may see at home or in a public shower or bathroom. There is no relationship between the way a penis appears when it is soft and when it is hard (erect).

## 7. Why does a boy's penis sometimes get hard when he is with a girl?

A boy's penis becomes hard when it is stimulated—often due to physical closeness to another person, or sexual thoughts, but sometimes for reasons that are not completely understood. Many boys find their penis erect upon awakening in the morning or when exposed to cold. Some boys have frequent erections. This is perfectly normal. As boys get older they find they have more control over their erections.

## 8. What causes homosexuality?

Most professionals no longer believe that homosexuality is a disease or a disorder. We are not sure why but about 10% of the population is homosexual. Recent evidence suggests that some people are born homosexual. Gay men and lesbian women exist in every culture and society.

In any case, we now know that homosexual experiences are not rare during childhood and adolescence. These experiences do not necessarily mean that a person will become an adult homosexual. Many young people who have had more than just a few homosexual experiences have been known to marry successfully. It is completely untrue that if you have homosexual thoughts or dreams you must be a homosexual. Mature people are aware of the fact that they have both homosexual and heterosexual feelings, even though the majority of them prefer sexual activities with members of the opposite sex. In this connection, you should know that one cannot judge by appearance whether a person is a homosexual.

It is wrong to discriminate against homosexuals in any way. People who make fun of, or worse yet, physically attack gays and lesbians obviously don't understand the facts and act out of ignorance or insecurity about their own sexual feelings.

## 9. What is "safe sex"?

No sex with anyone. "Safer sex" is no sex unless the female uses a birth control and the male uses a condom. No form of birth control or STD prevention is 100% safe, but not using them is 100% risk.

## 10. How come most parents don't tell their children about sex?

Some parents think that knowledge is harmful: "If you tell children about sex, they'll do it."

Some parents think that sex is dirty.

Some parents wait too long before they talk about it, and when they do, their children are unwilling or are too embarrassed to listen. Many parents simply do not know what to say or how much to say about sex.

If parents are askable, children ask questions at three, four and five years of age. It's about time parents realized that they are the main sex educators of their children, whether they do it well or badly. They might as well do a good job of it and begin by telling the truth!

# Conclusion

A lot of young people ask me if orgasm is the main thing in sex. Usually girls are the only ones who are supposed to have trouble reaching orgasm (climax). It is not generally known, but the fact is that boys do not always have an orgasm during ejaculation. Often they do, but not always—and the orgasm varies in strength and pleasure. Both men and women are able to enjoy sex without orgasm. It is rare for a couple to have orgasms at the same time during their first experiences. Some couples never have mutual orgasms. Couples who have healthy sexual attitudes and who are not overly concerned about their orgasms enjoy sex the most. Besides we need to get away from seeing sex as a kind of gymnastics. If I were to think of the ten most important aspects of a marital relationship, love, caring and intimacy would be number one; two, a sense of humor; three, honest communication; nine, sexual fulfillment; ten, sharing household tasks. What, in your opinion, would be numbers 4, 5, 6, 7, and 8?

I hope this book has been helpful. If you want to know more about sex, the following list of books and pamphlets will guide you. If, for some reason, you are still worried about sex and your parents have not been able to help you, ask your parents to arrange a meeting with a psychologist or a doctor who specializes in adolescent problems. If you feel you cannot talk to your parents at first, try talking to a sympathetic school counselor or teacher. You can also contact Planned Parenthood or a "hot line" in your community. Once you know and understand sex, it becomes just one part of life.

Remember, too, that being masculine for boys and feminine for girls means a great deal more than sexual intercourse. Most of all it means feeling secure. It means accepting yourself for what you are and having faith in what you can become. It means no one can make you feel inferior without your consent.

# SELECTED MATERIALS

## For Teenagers and Young Adults

*When Living Hurts* by Sol Gordon. The author describes this book as his most personal and most spiritual work. Consists of poems, essays, slogans. (Dell, 1989)

*The Teenage Survival Book* by Sol Gordon. Designed to communicate essential life knowledge and enhance self-acceptance among youth. New edition. (Times Books, 1991)

*Why Love Is Not Enough* by Sol Gordon. For people who are eager to make up their own minds about how to live and what risks are worth taking in relationships. (Bob Adams, 1990)

## For Younger Children and Teenagers
## Available from Prometheus Books

*Girls Are Girls and Boys Are Boys: So What's the Difference?* Sol Gordon's nonsexist liberating sex education book for children aged six to ten. Stunning illustrations by Vivien Cohen.

*Did the Sun Shine Before You Were Born?: A Sex Education Primer* by Sol and Judith Gordon. Paperback for children aged three to seven. Developed to help parents communicate facts about sex, reproduction and the family to their children. Illustrated by Vivien Cohen.

*A Better Safe than Sorry Book* by Sol and Judith Gordon. A sexual assault prevention paperback, designed for children aged three to nine as well as for concerned parents and professionals. Includes a parents' guide, designed to help parents feel more comfortable in their role as primary sex educators of their children. Illustrated by Vivien Cohen.

*Seduction Lines Heard 'Round the World and Answers You Can Give* by Sol Gordon. A witty, practical guide for teenagers that provides a variety of answers to extricate anyone from tedious, often embarrassing situations. Illustrated by Rita Fecher.

# For Professionals, Group Leaders and Parents

*Personal Issues in Human Sexuality* by Sol Gordon and Craig Snyder. A textbook for college students designed to help them examine and understand sexuality. (Allyn & Bacon, Inc., 1986)

*One Miracle at a Time* by Irving Dickman, with Sol Gordon. A paperback designed to answer the hundreds of questions parents have about raising a child with a handicap. (Fireside, 1992)

*Raising a Child Conservatively in a Sexually Permissive World* by Sol and Judith Gordon. A sensitive paperback about sexuality in the family. Stresses the role of self-esteem in healthy personality development and approaches the notion of "conservative" from a rational perspective. (Fireside, 1989)

*An End to Shame: Shaping Our Next Sexual Revolution* by Ira Reiss, Ph.D., with Harriet M. Reiss. A direct and challenging analysis of America's sexual problems that deals with such important issues as sex education for children, teenage sex, rape, AIDS, pornography, and sex therapy. (Prometheus Books, 1990)

**Audio-Visuals**
**Available from ETR Associates**
**P.O. Box 1830**
**Santa Cruz, CA 95061**

*How Can I Tell if I'm Really in Love?* A nonpreaching videocassette that speaks to kids in their own language. Dr. Sol Gordon, with the help of actors from TV's hit shows, "Family Ties," "Cheers" and "Valerie," helps teenagers evaluate intimate relationships.

*Strong Kids, Safe Kids.* A critically acclaimed and award-winning videocassette that teaches children and concerned adults the basic skills that can help prevent child sexual abuse and abduction. Hosted by Henry Winkler of the hit TV series, "Happy Days," this video intersperses serious advice by Dr. Sol Gordon and Kee MacFarlane with music, delightful humor and animation.

*On Being Gay: A Conversation with Brian McNaught.* A two-part, eighty-minute videocassette, which presents, and then dispels, the common misconceptions about homosexuality and deals with McNaught's experience of growing up gay in America.

# More About AIDS

AIDS is a fatal disease. You can get it from sex and sharing needles (such as those used by drug addicts). You cannot get this disease from hugging, holding hands or being near someone with AIDS.

Some people think AIDS is a disease of gay people but this is not true. You can get it from all kinds of sexual behavior—anal, oral and vaginal sex. In the United States more than 125,000 people (as of 1992) have already died from AIDS.

A person may get the disease from a single contact with an infected person. But the symptoms (signs) may not show up for as long as 10 years. That's why a lot of people who test HIV positive (the common name of the virus that causes AIDS) may appear perfectly healthy. They can still spread the disease. Many symptoms of AIDS can also occur in healthy people who do not have AIDS. Simple medical tests can identify the source of most infections. Don't take chances with your health. If you have had any risky sexual experiences or used IV drugs, get tested—not just once but every six months for many years to come.

It is better to wait until you are married before having sex and even then you need to be sure of the person you are marrying.

If you are not going to listen to me—whenever you have sex use protection.

# Some Thoughts And Definitions Of Love

"Love is not boastful, or conceited, or rude; love is patient, kind, and without envy."

I Corinthians

X 111, 14

"When the satisfaction or security of another person becomes as significant to one as is one's own satisfaction or security, then the state of love exists."

Harry Stack Sullivan, Psychiatrist

"The most unsatisfactory men are those who pride themselves on their virility and regard sex as if it were some sort of athletics at which you win cups. It is a woman's spirit and mood a man has to stimulate in order to make sex interesting. The real lover is the man who can thrill you by just touching your hand and smiling into your eyes."

Marilyn Monroe, *My Story*

"The tragic mistake is to assume that any treasure, person, or object, must be possessed to be loved."

Ethel Sabin Smith

"Love is the overwhelming desire and persistent effort of one person to create for another person the condition which that other person can become the man or woman God meant them to be."

William H. Genne, Theologian

"The only abnormality is the incapacity to love."

Anais Nin

"It has been wisely said that we cannot really love anybody at whom we never laugh."

Agnes Repplier. *Reader's Digest*, Aug. 1962

"The truth is that there is only one terminal dignity — Love. And the story of a love is not important. What is important is that one is capable of love. It is perhaps the only glimpse we are permitted of eternity."

Helen Hayes. *Guideposts*, Jan., 1960.

Here are some promotion of self esteem ideas from my *Teenage Survival Book;* If you feel good about yourself, you are not available to be used by others.

- Risk intimacy by telling people about yourself.

- If you can't be anything you want to be, at least don't be anything you don't want to be.

- If you have a tendency to put yourself down, don't tell anyone. It's really boring to be with someone who does this.

- If you have advice to give, don't expect anyone to follow it easily (or at all). When was the last time someone told you "not to worry" and you stopped?

- If you do something wrong, you should feel guilty. Mature guilt is organizing, but not long-lasting. You will either make amends or you won't do it again.

- If you feel guilty about something that doesn't make sense —like having "evil" thoughts—your guilt will disorganize you and be the energy for repeating the unacceptable thoughts (obsessions) or behavior (compulsions) over and over again.

- If your love for another person is mature, this love will energize you and help you to feel optimistic about your-self. If your love is immature it will exhaust you, and bring on feelings of depression, anger, and jealousy.

- If you want to change a behavior of yours (such as talking too much) your first efforts at change must be forced and mechanical. This is because the unacceptable behavior

43

has become a "natural response (a habit) to tension. By forcing an opposite response (such as not talking so much) you will be "rewarded" by enormous rushes of anxiety. If you can handle the "mechanical" changes and the tension, you can develop a more acceptable "habit."

- If you notice that you are intolerant of someone else's behavior—like a person who is boasting a lot—and that person is not hurting you, it means that you are reacting to something about yourself that you don't like.

- The process of not doing what you are supposed to do is much more tiring than doing and getting the most boring tasks over with. The ultimate creative busyness is when you have time for almost everything you want to do.

- The criticism of someone you don't respect should have no impact on you. Life is too precious for you to be offended by or react to anybody's ridicule. Remember too, not everything you say or they say—or happens— is important. Select, don't settle.

And here's a good definition of self-esteem: "Appreciating my own worth and importance and having the character to be accountable for myself and to act responsibly toward others."
—California Legislative Task Force on
Self Esteem (1990)

# The Ten
Most Important
Parts of
# Marriage

1. Love, sensitivity and respect for each other
2. A sense of humor and playfulness
3. Honest communication without violating private thoughts and experiences
4. Doing meaningful things together
5. Sharing time with people who are really enjoyed, either together or singly
6. Not compromising who you are or want to be, or what you want to have, like children, a career, or faithfulness to each other
7. Tolerance for weak spots (like being tired, clumsy, irritable at times) and for opposite points of view
8. Acceptance of each other's likes and dislikes, and levels of energy
9. Sexual intercourse
10. Sharing household tasks

What else do you think is important?

# Signs of
## Immature Love

* You are tired most of the time
* Love seems more like a burden than a joy
* Violence is part of the relationship
* You keep having thoughts like "Maybe things will get better"
* Your partner frequently makes promises that aren't kept
* You feel

## *MISERABLE*

# Signs of
## Mature Love

* You have a lot of energy
* You have a sense of humor
* You really appreciate each other's ideas
* Neither of you *frequently* asks "Are you sure you love me?" "Do you really care about me?"
* When you are together, you spend most of your time enjoyably and creatively
* You can talk about each other's likes and dislikes
* You are a person, not a sex object
* You can spend a day alone with your partner (without television) and find it

## *FANTASTIC*